The Harvard Report

A STUDY OF THE SOUL MUSIC ENVIRONMENT PREPARED FOR COLUMBIA RECORDS GROUP

Dr. Logan H. Westbrooks

Ascent Book Publishing
1902 5th Avenue
Los Angeles, CA 90018
Loganwestbrooks.com

©2017 Dr. Logan H. Westbrooks

All rights reserved, including the right to reproduce this book or portion thereof in any form whatsoever without prior written permission of the publisher. No liability is assumed for any damages that may result from the use of information contained within.

Edited by Dee Robinson the RightWriter
Cover Design by Jessica Godbee

Printed in the United States of America

ISBN: 978-0-9987822-0-1

SAN: 990-0306

Library of Congress
Control Number: 2017937188

Dedication

To the Original 13…

INTRODUCTION

After almost 50 years, it's time to set the record straight. "A Study of the Soul Music Environment prepared for Columbia Records Group" or the *Harvard Report*, as it is called, has been discussed by many, maligned by some, and misunderstood by most.

It was, and still is, common practice for corporations—regardless of the industry—to research the markets before investing in them. The *Harvard Report* was one such study.

It was commissioned in 1972 by Columbia Records Group (CBS Records) to determine the feasibility and profitability of delving into Black Music Marketing. I was the liaison between CBS Records and Harvard Business School, and I have the original copy of the Harvard Report as it was presented to me.

The full report has never before been published, which conceivably contributed to its rise to mythical proportions ranging all the way from an outstanding business strategy to a sinister plot to take over Black music. For the first time, the *Harvard Report* can be read, analyzed, and picked apart allowing the readers to draw their own conclusions.

The report can now be studied based on information acquired by the researchers and an almost 50-year time span to compare the results of unintended or intentional consequences on the Black music market. Over that period of time, many superstar acts were established, fortunes made, and legendary songs created on a much broader scale than ever before because of the involvement of the distribution power of CBS Records.

Much has been written and spread over the internet about the *Harvard Report*, most of it misinformation. With the publication of this book, I think people will be surprised at what it was, and more importantly, what it wasn't.

A philosophical question arises about the ability of a small company's survival when partnering with a powerful corporation. Can they exist together in a symbiotic relationship or is it inevitable that one will be swallowed up by the other? Is it cultural appropriation or is it just business? You, the reader, can now decide.

HARVARD UNIVERSITY

GRADUATE SCHOOL OF BUSINESS ADMINISTRATION

GEORGE F. BAKER FOUNDATION

Soldiers Field
Boston, Massachusetts 02163
May 11, 1972

Logan H. Westbrooks

    The findings contained in this report are the result of an investigation of the Soul music environment and analyses of relevant data conducted by the Columbia Records Project Group. The analyses led to three major conclusions pertaining to Columbia's present and desired postures in the Soul music industry:

(1) A market opportunity for CRG exists in this area.
(2) CRG's previous efforts in Soul music have not been adequate.
(3) Several changes in CRG's organization and orientation will be required for success in the Soul music market.

    To expand on the above conclusions, it was estimated that a market of approximately $60 million at manufacturers' prices exists for Soul music recordings. CRG's previous efforts have been hampered by an organization staffed by personnel oriented to the popular music field which differs fundamentally from Soul music in the critical factors required for success. In order to become a significant factor in the Soul music industry, CRG must establish an internal Soul music group and improve the quality of Soul music product released on recordings.

Respectfully submitted,

Creative Marketing Strategy
Columbia Records Project Group

THE HARVARD REPORT

I. INTRODUCTION
   Purpose
   Scope
   Major Conclusions

II. ANALYSIS
   Definition of the Market
   Size
   Historical Development
   Evolution of Soul
   Impact on Other Sectors of Popular Music Culture
   Role of Specialized National Companies in
      Broadening this Market
   Internal Dynamics
   Airplay/Playlists/Crossover
   Payola
   Competition
   Analysis of Columbia Records Group

III. RECOMMENDATION AND RATIONALE

IV. PLAN OF ACTION

V. ADDENDUM

I. INTRODUCTION

Purpose

The objectives of this study were:

1. To examine the feasibility of an expanded Columbia Record Group (CRG) Soul program.
2. To evaluate CRG's present organization in the context of the requirements for that expansion.
3. To examine the implications of such an explanation for CRG from strategic as well as financial perspectives.

Scope

The Soul segment of the music market has been analyzed from the standpoint of its historical development, its internal dynamics, and its relationship to the broader world of contemporary music. CRG's general approach to the music industry has been reviewed, with particular reference to its efforts to date in the Soul market.

This study has confronted limitations inherent to any quantitatively-oriented analysis of the record industry: the sources of information are limited and widely dispersed. Despite these limitations, the degree of uncertainty associated with the resultant conclusions is not inordinately high.

Major Conclusion

The primary conclusions resulting from the study are:

1. A market opportunity exists in the Soul segment of the music market.
2. CRG's past efforts to cultivate this market have lacked virtually all of the elements critical for success.
3. To capitalize on that market opportunity, CRG must significantly modify and substantially broaden its current efforts to cultivate that market.

II. ANALYSIS

Definition of the Soul Market

A definition of the Soul market is critical both to the determination of its size and composition. The issue is very complex, and there is no generally accepted definition. Efforts to define it in terms of a 'certain sound' lack precision. Defining it in terms of specific artists can be problematic because a given artist may produce a Soul record one day, and a Rock record the next. At the same time, artists do manifest tendencies in one or another direction. A rough typology based upon three broad tendencies is one way to suggest the Soul market's boundaries:

SOUL CONTENT OF ARTIST'S REPERTOIRE		
Almost All	Mixed	Almost None
James Brown	Isaac Hayes	Miles Davis
Wilson Picket	Joe Williams	Johnny Mathis
Aretha Franklin	Roberta Flack	Gloria Lynn
The Chi-Lites	Fifth Dimension	Mills Brothers
Clara Ward Singers	Sly & the Family Stone	Thelonious Monk
Joe Tex	Lou Rawls	Dionne Warwick

Another way of getting at the definition of Soul is by enumerating some of its features:

- It is characterized in many instances by a raw, driving beat that is as much viscerally as aurally experienced.

- It enjoys great popularity among Black people.

- It is generally though not exclusively produced by Black artists.

Finally, from the standpoint of convenience, it can be defined as the kind of music which is likely to appear on Billboard's "Soul" Chart, and the kind of music likely to be programmed on Black listener-oriented radio stations such as WILD Boston, WWRL New York, WJMO Cleveland, WVON Chicago and KGFJ Los Angeles.

Size

Beyond the problem of market definition lie difficulties in quantifying the market because of the virtual absence of relevant published data. None of the companies in the Soul market, nor in the entire record industry, for that matter, are free-standing, publicly-owned. They are either subsidiaries or divisions of conglomerates, or privately held. As a consequence, published information is scarce. The sources analyzed (Appendix A) suggest a market on the order of $60 million at manufacturers' prices, broken down as follows:

Albums	$30 million
Singles	$30 million

Factory prices of $2.50 and $0.50 for albums and singles respectively yield this unit price for the market:

Albums	12 million
Singles	60 million

The size of the total recorded music market has been estimated at $1,660 million for 1970. Since that figure is based upon average 'suggested retail price,' it is necessary to convert Soul albums and singles into equivalent figures, $5.50 and $0.90 respectively, to determine Soul's share of the total recorded music market:

Albums	$66 million
Singles	$54 million
TOTAL	$120 million

$120 million/$1,660 million = 7.23%

This estimate is considered to be on the conservative side, since it excludes those sales of artists in the 'Mixed' category, which are considered more in the Rock than Soul area. A less restrictive approach would probably assign a total market share on the order of 10% to Soul music.

Historical Development of Soul Music Market

For the purposes of this analysis, there are three broad trends in the historical development of Soul music which are especially relevant:

1. There has been an evolution of Soul from a series of isolated, local-regional styles, sounds, and artists towards a more homogeneous and stylized sound almost national in the scope of its popularity among Blacks. And with this has come the emergence of Black artists with a national following within the Black community.
2. Soul music has had a significant and continuing influence on other sectors of the popular music culture in the United States and Great Britain, initially through the medium of White artists who first covered, then later interpreted Soul music for White audiences. Ultimately this influence broadened through the medium of Black Soul artists themselves as they belatedly received exposure and access to White audiences.
3. Aggressive, innovative, specialized national companies highly focused on Soul, have played a key role in broadening the market for Soul music both inside and outside the Black community.

The historic disinterest in the Black record buying market by the major record companies gave rise to a tier of small independent record companies which catered to it. At that time, the Black market consisted of local/regional audiences with particular tastes.

The companies which emerged in a given region tended to concentrate particularly on styles with local associations. These independents were small and almost always seriously under-capitalized. They relied almost entirely on the ingenuity of their owners, who functioned as their own talent scouts, producers, promoters and distributors.

They were essentially running their record companies out of the back trunks of their cars. Operating from a small and uncertain base, they had few resources with which to expand their operations. Almost all of the important ones attempted to break into the national market.

Not until 1953 did one of these succeed in reaching the White market with a Black vocal group. 'Jubilee' made this breakthrough with its 'Crying in the Chapel,' by the Orioles, which made the Pop music Top Twenty. By and large, however, these independents had short life cycles. Even the ones who were able to survive, such as Atlantic, suffered because they did not have the resources with which to expand their promotional and distribution networks. Thus, local hits remained that: local hits, because of the difficulties in achieving more exposure.

The treatment of Black artists and writers by the major record companies during this period can be described as racist. Cover versions of R&B hits by White artists were common practice in the 1940s and 1950s. As an example, many of Elvis Presley's hits in the 1950s, when he was a dominant force on the music scene, were nothing but cover versions of hits in the then fairly small Black market.

The lack of interest in the Black market exhibited by the major record companies also had implications for Black artists. It meant that unless a Black artist was willing to sever his ties with Black music, and instead work in the field of popular music, he would be unable to gain wide exposure.

The disinterest in Black music was not, however, universal. In the 1950s Decca had an interest in Black music. It was in fairly close touch with tastes and styles in the market and evidently appreciated the potential of the music. Mercury, too, participated in this market. But in contrast to the activity of these two companies, the reaction of RCA, Columbia, Capital and MGM to Black music was almost total indifference.

Internal Dynamics

An examination of how the record music market works, from the point at which a record is released by a record company, to the point at which the consumer makes his purchase reveals that radio is the critical link. For the record to sell, it must receive exposure; practically speaking, that means that the record be played on the radio. To do that, the record must get on a playlist.

What looks like an unbreakable circle is involved here, since one of the principal ways a record can get on a playlist is by generating sales. What provides the break in the circle is that part of the playlist which is set aside for new releases which the program director considers to have "hit potential." And it is this part of the playlist which becomes the target for all of the record promoters.

There is a very important difference between Top 40 and other types of stations, such as Soul and Easy Listening, with respect to this discretionary part of the playlist. The difference is that it is much easier to promote a new release on to a Soul and Easy Listening playlist on the strength of the product, the artist or the promoter, before that record has received any airplay.

The discretionary part of Top 40 playlists, on the other hand, is more often selected from among those new releases which have gotten on and stayed on other playlists, such as Soul. A recent study of the record industry underscores that point: "Approximately 30 percent of the records heard over Top 40 stations are selected from "down home" Blues programming of the Negro oriented stations found in most major cities, which program strictly "Rhythm and Blues" stations, it is likely to be co-opted by the Top 40 programmers and exposed to their wider audience.

The Negro audience thus serves as a test market for many of the selections that reach the Top 40 stations. Records having strong sales in the ghetto record stores as a result of airplay over R&B stations will soon be heard by Top 40 listeners."[1]

This is not to suggest that new releases are impossible to promote onto a Top 40 playlist before they have made other playlists since new releases of established artists, especially when they are following up on a recent hit, are almost certain to get some, and perhaps considerable, airplay unless the record is poor. The record company can create interest in a new record and anticipation for it by heavily promoting and advertising it before it is released.

The fact that 30 percent of the Top 40 is composed of records which have "crossed-over" from Soul stations underscores the strategic importance of Soul stations as one of the most effective vehicles for getting onto the Top 40. What this means is that the competition among promoters for Soul airplay involves far more than simply the prospect of record sales to Black consumers.

In sum, Soul radio is of strategic importance to the record companies for two principal reasons: first, it provides access to a large and growing record buying public, namely, the Black consumer. Second, and for some of the record companies more important, it is perhaps the most effective way of getting a record to a Top 40 playlist.

The critical importance of Black radio for the reasons just mentioned, coupled with the fact that Black DJs still have some, though diminishing discretion in the selection of records to be played, and the widely shared belief that Black DJs are seriously underpaid has led to widely held beliefs within the industry that payola is pervasive in Black radio.

Until recently, Black radio was considered to be the last remaining pocket of payola. A recent Jack Anderson article, however, suggests that if anything, payola is pervasive throughout the entire record industry. Anderson's article has generated considerable discussion from the industry and the government, and the issue is likely to remain alive for at least several months.

With respect to payola in Black radio, this study has identified considerable suspicion, but no evidence. Payola, of course, is difficult to document. This study cannot conclude that there is no payola in Black radio. It can be concluded, however, that some of the assumptions concerning payola might usefully be examined:

There have been important changes in Black radio in that there is a growing trend toward professionalization.

1. There is not as much of a discrepancy between the salaries that White and Black DJs receive, as was formerly the case.

2. The playlists of Black radio stations are getting tighter, and DJs have diminishing discretion over what is played.

3. More careful distinctions must be made between those expenses which can be considered legitimate business related expenses, and those which are nothing more than subtle forms of payola.

4. Though payola may now and in the foreseeable future continue to be a significant problem for those companies interested in cultivating this market, but unwilling to violate Federal Anti-Bribery Act to do so, it is not a decisive one.

The recent Anderson article, coupled with the immediate industry reaction, underscored the industry's reluctance to call attention to itself and to face another government investigation. This situation is likely to provoke caution and to put radio on its best behavior over the short run, at least, as a way of warding off new government investigation and legislation.

For companies interested in cultivating the Soul market, but unwilling to participate in the more obvious forms of payola, the time would appear to be opportune to move into this market. Whatever payola problems there are, are likely to be less salient until this current payola discussion declines.

The major internal dynamics of the industry may be summarized as follows:

1. The importance of Black radio as an avenue of access into the Black consumer market, and as a springboard into the Top 40 Charts through the phenomenon of crossover, is likely to continue. In the case of the latter, it is likely to increase to the extent that Top 40 playlists become even <u>tighter</u> and <u>shorter</u>.

2. In the short run, industry and government scrutiny of payola in the record business is likely to drive what payola there is deeper underground and reduce its immediate importance as a key obstacle in Black radio. In the long run, the growing professionalization of Black radio, and the increasing specialization between the DJ and Program Director functions is likely at least to change the locus of payola, and ultimately to reduce its overall importance.

3. While this study is inconclusive regarding the form and volume of payola in Black radio, it does conclude that, while undoubtedly a formidable obstacle, payola is not an insurmountable one, and that a persistent and politic promotional force, using good public relations and consistently high quality product can probably go a long way toward overcoming the obstacles posed by payola for companies who are not willing to engage in that practice.

Competition

An expanded CRG Soul program will have to compete for the limited available airplay with three types of firms:

1. Specialized national companies, principally Motown, Atlantic and Stax

2. Major national record companies, such as RCA, Capitol, MCA

3. Smaller independents

The specialized national companies will provide the most formidable competition. They have an entrenched position and control half of the total market. They have most of the established Soul artists. Their management and professional staffs have extensive experience in this market, and a deep understanding of its subtleties. They operate through a highly sophisticated personal and informational network which they have built up over a period of many years.

Finally, they have a profound understanding of the art form with which they work, and of its commercial possibilities. In fact, they have helped to shape it, thus are in a position to change and manipulate it while the rest of the competitors can only react to its seemingly unpredictable evolution.

CRG can expect to find itself in competition with these firms in markets which CRG presently dominates as these firms, their base in Soul well established, graduate their artists into other markets, such as the Middle of the Road and Pop.

A dominant position in Soul has provided these companies with the financial and management resources, and the consumer visibility to broaden their product lines and move into other, related markets.

This underlines another element of the Soul market's importance. In a sense, it has provided these firms with the base from which to challenge the majors in other segments of the popular music market.

Second in importance will be the other major national firms which, like CRG, can be considered late-comers into this market. In the short run, should CRG decide to expand, it will find itself in competition with these firms for the limited available Black professional and management personnel who are experienced in this area. It will also find itself in competition for available Black artists, especially from those companies which may be out to "cream this market" rather than build for the future.

CRG should not find itself at any particular disadvantage with respect to these firms. It will find that they are as uninitiated and uninformed about this market as it is. Thus, an expanded CRG Soul program could quickly achieve a decided advantage over other major record companies entering this market if it did something they are not likely to do: to put together a well thought out, well planned and well financed initiative aimed at long term market penetration, rather than short term profits from an opportunistic "creaming" program.

It could also achieve an edge by providing its Soul initiative with the flexible decision making capability which its major record company competitors are not likely to have.

The small independents will represent more of an opportunity for CRG than a competitive threat. An expanded CRG program might well look to these small independents for a number of things which could strengthen its overall position.

These small independents could provide a source of product, in the form of "hot masters;" talent which could have national potential; experienced personnel for CRG's staff, in the areas of promotion and production; and serve as a source of captive independent producers. Finally, CRG, with broadened distribution in the Black community, which an expanded Soul program would bring, could serve as a distribution arm for their proprietary product under a custom label program.

Analysis of Columbia

There are two facts which must be taken into account in examining CRG's present capabilities for broadening its Soul efforts:

1. This market has never been important to CRG. It has never systematically cultivated it.

2. Its incursions into this market, as with the Okeh and Date labels, have been sporadic, half-hearted and short-lived.

As a consequence, CRG knows little about Black consumers, Soul artists, and Black professionals in the music and related businesses, such as radio. Aside from isolated White professionals in its organization, it has little knowledge about how this market works.

It is not tied into the strategic sources of information about what is happening inside that market. And the almost total absence of Blacks at the professional and managerial levels in its organization until recently has denied it of what could have been a valuable resource for relating to that market.

CRG's historic neglect of the Soul market has brought upon it some problems in respect to its image in this market. Interviews with people in the Soul music business indicate that CRG is perceived as an ultra-rich, ultra-white giant which has for the most part chosen to snub Blacks in the business. Blacks in the trade feel that CRG has heaped upon them the ultimate insult; that of ignoring their existence.

Even when the slight involved seemingly superficial things (CRG fails to invite them to functions; DJs say they do not get free tickets to shows from CRG as do White DJs) these are seen as manifestations of a broader pattern. Further, they perceive a degree of arrogance in CRG promotion personnel who try to get airplay for a Soul product viewed by Black radio personnel as sub-standard. That these promotion personnel until recently were almost always White did not help matters.

Given CRG's present situation, an expansion in its Soul program aimed at establishing a dominant position for it in the Soul market would require a significant financial investment and organizational commitment. Time would be needed to build a base organization and to get it functioning as a cohesive unit. Experienced Soul personnel would have to be hired in the areas of A&R, production and promotion.

The present Soul roster would have to be enriched and promoted more heavily. This program could involve significant talent recruitment and development costs. Time would be needed to build productive working relationships with the trades, and with Soul radio personnel to open up the channels for the promotion and distribution of Columbia's Soul product.

Time and money would be required to sift through a variety of independent producers in order to single out those with whom a long-term relationship might be compatible. Considerable experimentation might be required to sort out an authentic, commercially viable, reproducible, and distinct Columbia sound. Such a venture aimed at long-term market penetration would probably incur losses for several years before achieving profitability.

III. RATIONALE

This raises the question of whether CRG should undertake such an expansion. The major conclusion of this study is that it should do so for several reasons:

1. The potential for profitability could be significant. Exhibit 1, based upon a level of activity provided for in Exhibit 2, estimates that the Soul program should achieve Break-Even within three years, and an Operating Profit of $1,401K by the fifth year.

2. The time is opportune. Whatever pressures there are for payola in Black radio will probably subside in the short-run, perhaps long enough to allow CRG to broaden its participation in Soul.

3. As the dominant firm in the recording industry, there is no reason why Columbia should forfeit any segment of the total market to its competitors. The Soul music market is not inconsequential. As noted above, it represents roughly seven percent of the total recorded music sales at the retail level. At the present time, CRG has but two artists, Sly and Santana, who get on Soul Charts with any consistency. And it is important to realize that they get on Soul Charts more as Rock acts crossing over into Soul, rather than as Soul entries. These two acts aside, CRG has but two or three artists with significant Soul potential.

4. Soul music has broad national appeal which extends far beyond Black consumers. <u>Billboard's</u> "Hot 100" which is based predominantly upon a sample of White-consumer-oriented retail outlets, will rarely have as few as 20, and can have as many as 35 records on any given week which also appear on <u>Billboard's</u> "Soul" Chart consisting of the Top 50 Soul hits. In short, CRG's miniscule program not only deprives it of product for Black consumers, but also limits its ability to compete within the full range of the "Hot 100."

5. It is a commentary on Columbia's strength that it is able to maintain its dominant position on the "Hot 100" even though it has virtually no entries for a music segment which constitutes roughly one third of that chart. A successfully expanded Soul program would strengthen CRG's already dominant position on the "Hot 100" to the point of making it practically invincible.

6. Soul radio stations offer the most effective and most direct way of getting on Top 40. This will become even more true as Top 40 playlists become tighter. By remaining marginal to this market, CRG is denying itself of one of the most direct routes for getting certain kinds of records onto Top 40.

7. Soul music is one of the very few basic art forms which is indigenous to America, although its own roots may be traced to

Africa. It has been, and probably will continue to be, a vital and influential force on contemporary popular music. And Soul is by no means a static music form.

It too will continue to change. Companies able to work successfully in this art form will be in a position to relate more dynamically to its impact on other forms of popular music, such as Pop and Rock. This will be especially important as these three music styles converge upon one another.

IV. PLAN OF ACTION

Recommended Strategy

The recommended strategy encompasses three broad areas:

1. Expand external sources of product by augmenting present custom label activity and increasing outside product resources.

2. Develop an internal means of Soul music product generation.

3. Establish a semi-autonomous Soul music product group.

The recommendations provide a means for immediate expansion of CRG's activities in the Soul music market, and a basis for coordinated, broader scale future action. The suggested actions will enable CRG to become exposed to more product offerings from varied sources while developing the internal capability to evaluate, cultivate, and promote Soul music talent.

This expansion of quality product offerings and intensified efforts in the solicitation of product will establish CRG's interest in Soul music to industry members, and contribute to the creation of a more desirable image within the industry. Consequently, increased lines of communication will be opened with industry product sources.

Two alternative sets of recommendations were considered. The first was the acquisition of a company presently strong in the Soul music business. This strategy is not a feasible one for Columbia for the following reasons:

1. The dominance of the CBS organization in the communications and entertainment industry could possibly precipitate anti-trust action if it were to attempt the acquisition of a major company in the music industry.

2. Of the three companies strong enough to offer Columbia a base from which to operate, Atlantic has been bought out by the Kinney group, Stax was acquired by Gulf and Western, and it is rumored that Motown is not in a position to contemplate an acquisition at this time.

The second alternative, which was the acquiring of presently established talent was similarly discounted because of the following:

1. The costs of acquiring such talent would be high (it is rumored that Wilson Pickett had announced his availability for $500,000).

2. There is a risk that the performer may not produce for Columbia at expected levels of quality.

3. The base structure required to support top talent does not exist within CRG at this time. This approach would, therefore, necessitate a

delay until the proper internal support has been established at CRG.

4. An approach such as this might precipitate competitive reaction if pursued vigorously.

5. The payment of significant dollar amounts to newly signed talent might lead to jealousies among artists presently under contract and escalation of their money demands.

Recommended Organization

The analysis of the Soul music industry indicates that the following functions will be critical to the success of CRG's Soul Music Group:

1. Decision making responsibility and authority for talent signings and product acquisition. Implicit in this is the assumption that the group will have an adequate budget.

2. Independent evaluation of Soul music talent and product.

3. Capability for arranging product and coordinating artist's activities within the specialized context of the Soul music form.

4. Establishment and maintenance of beneficial relationships with Soul music radio stations and dealers.

5. Coordination of Soul music sales activities with the existing sales force.

6. Integration of the Soul music group with other functional activities within Columbia, which will be necessary for support (e.g. legal, advertising, physical production, sales).

The formal organization as shown in Exhibit 4 would consist of a Director of the Soul music group, an Administrative Coordinator, Manager of National Promotion, Manager of A&R, National Sales Coordinator, two product managers, three secretaries, and twelve field promotional men.

Responsibilities

DIRECTOR OF SOUL MUSIC GROUP – would be responsible for overall coordination and management of group activities and for decisions involving talent signings and product acquisition. In addition, budget responsibility for the group would be held in this position.

ADMINISTRATIVE COORDINATOR – would act as integrative liaison between the group, and other companies within Columbia Records Group. Also would control administrative arrangements internal to the group.

MANAGER OF NATIONAL PROMOTION – would be responsible for directing the efforts of the twelve field promotional men toward the establishment of relationships with Soul music radio stations, and dealers, and the coordination of national promotional campaigns.

MANAGER OF A&R – would perform the functions of seeking out, evaluating and developing Soul music talent. In addition, this person would handle artist relationships.

NATIONAL SALES COODINATOR – would coordinate the sales effort for Soul product with the present sales force which would be used to distribute Soul music product.

PRODUCT MANAGER – the two product managers would arrange for the packaging and merchandising of Soul product, plan national promotional campaigns for the Soul artist, and work closely with the promotional staff in their implementation.

FIELD PROMOTIONAL FORCE – would consist of four regional and eight local promotion men, and would be responsible for maintenance of relationships with Soul music radio stations, distributors, and retailers.

The proposed organization is not intended to be an additional internal label, but rather a coordinating activity for Soul product which will be able to release artists on any of the Columbia labels. The intention is not to establish rigid guidelines for the handling of Soul music artists, but rather to create the proper atmosphere for the kind of music being produced by the artist.

For example, it is conceivable that a given artist might have one record arranged, produced, and promoted through the Soul music group, and the next through the existing organization, depending on the nature of the sound.

However, overall responsibility for an artist should be specifically assigned to one of the Columbia Records Group organizations at all times, to minimize lapses in the artist's development. In the case of talent presently under contract, the desires of the artist in addition to the sound should be considered before the decision is made on which group handles the product.

The Soul music group should be semi-autonomous with the Director reporting to the President of CRG. This arrangement will provide the flexibility determined to be so important in earlier sections of this report, while manifesting top management commitment to the Soul music business.

In addition, the independent nature of the group will eliminate potential conflicts resulting from having to work within an environment which does not include an understanding of either the Soul music art form or the requirements for success in this business.

Implementation

The adoption of the recommended strategy is intended to be accomplished in three phases:

1. During phase one, emphasis should be placed on establishment of market position by expanding the existing custom label operation.

2. In phase two, market position should be further established, and industry reputation developed by utilizing more externally generated product.

3. When the third phase is reached, emphasis should be placed on internal product, and the development of a distinctive Soul music sound for Columbia.

The three phases are not intended to be mutually exclusive, but rather interactive and continuous as shown by Exhibit 5. The purpose of this sequential arrangement is to indicate to the industry Columbia's interest in Soul music, and thereby attract more talent and product while providing some initial operating results.

The three-phase approach is in effect a tactic of BUYING TIME WHILE THE REQUIRED INTERNAL SUPPORT ORGANIZATION IS STAFFED AND DEVELOPED.

An added benefit will be the opportunity for acclimatization of the present CRG organization while the Soul music group is being gradually developed. During this period, an educational process can be started which will be directed toward the minimization of organizational problems.

EXHIBIT 1

YEAR	1	2	3	4	5
MARKET SIZE	$60MM	64MM	69MM	74MM	79MM
ESTIMATED LEVEL OF MARKET PENETRATION	2%	4%	5%	7%	10%
CONTRIBUTION AVAILABLE	$559K	1,193K	1,608K	2,433K	3,711K
LESS:					
FIXED COSTS	$830K	870K	915K	960K	1,010K
DIRECT COSTS	300K	500K	650K	900K	1,300K
	1,130K	1,370K	1,565K	1,860K	2,310K
OPERATING PROFIT (LOSS)	(571K)	(177K)	43K	573K	1,401K
CUMULATIVE PROFIT (LOSS)	(571K)	(748)	(705K)	(132K)	1,269K

Assumptions:

1. Market will grow at a compounded annual rate of 7%.
2. CRG will achieve a 5–1 singles-albums ratio for the first three years, and a 4-1 ratio for years 4 and 5.
3. Fixed costs will increase at the rate of 5% per year.

EXHIBIT 2

PROPOSED ANNUAL OPERATING BUDGET

1. FIELD PERSONNEL:

Regional Directors (4) @ $60K	$240K
Promotion/Sales Personnel (8) @ $25K	200K

    (These figures include salary, fringe benefits, travel, entertainment, and all other expenses required to support a professional staff man in the field. CRG sources indicate travel and entertainment expenses amount to roughly three times salary for Regional Directors, and roughly one and one-half times salary for other professional staff.)

2. HEADQUARTERS PERSONNEL:

7 Professional Staff, including Director of Special Markets, National Promotion Director, Manager of A&R, National Sales Coordinator, 2 Product Managers and Administrative Coordinator	210K

    (These figures include salary, fringe benefits, travel, entertainment and other related expenses.)

3 Clerical/Secretarial @ $10K	30K

3. OTHER HEADQUARTERS EXPENSES — 50K

4. DISCRETIONARY BUDGET FOR TALENT DEVELOPMENT — 100K

    Total $830K

5. RECORDING, PRODUCT PREPARATION AND PROMOTION COSTS:

Year	1	2	3	4	5
	$300K	500K	650K	900K	1,300K

NOTES TO EXHIBITS I AND II

1. Unit contributions are assumed to be as follows:

	Singles	Albums
Factory Price	.53	2.50
Less: Variable Costs	.30	1.25
Contribution	.23	1.25

<u>Variable costs</u> are of two types: 1) those variable to <u>manufacturing</u>, which includes manufacturing, warehousing, plant returns, transportation and obsolescence, 2) and those variable to <u>selling</u>, which includes artist and copyright royalties, union fees, sales commission and cooperative advertising.

<u>Contribution</u> is defined as sales revenue less variable costs.

2. Contributions for the several singles-album ratio at the different levels of market penetration is computed by dividing sales revenues by the appropriate weighted sales figure, and then multiplying the resultant figure by the weighted contribution. Weighted sales and contribution figures are derived as follows:

Singles/Albums Ratio	1-1	3-1	5-1	7-1
Singles sales	.53	1.59	2.65	3.71
Album sales	2.50	2.50	2.50	2.50
Weighted sales	3.03	4.09	5.15	6.21
Singles contribution	.23	.69	1.15	1.61
Album contribution	1.25	1.25	1.25	1.25
Weighted contribution	1.48	1.94	2.40	2.86

Thus, if market penetration = 5%, and singles-albums ration = 3-1

$60MM x 5% = $3MM
$3MM / 4.09 = 733.5K Aggregate units
733.5K x 1.94 = 1.423MM
Total Contribution = 1.423MM

3. The proposed Operating Budget includes two categories of costs: First, those <u>Fixed costs</u> which are <u>incremental</u> to CRG as a result of the expanded Soul program. Thus, it does not include an allocation to general corporate overhead. Second, <u>Direct costs</u>, which include <u>recording costs</u>, such as studio time and talent costs; <u>album preparation</u>; and <u>advertising and promotion</u> expenses such as trade and radio promotion peculiar to a specific product. CRG's estimates, based upon historical experiences, is that they average roughly half of variable costs. In light of the start-up character of the proposed Soul programs, and the likelihood that these Direct costs, in relation to Variable costs, will exceed CRG's historical average, at least initially, an alternate method for dealing with these costs has been used. Funds have been budgeted based upon probable level of recording and promotional activity.

4. <u>Operating profit</u> is profit before interest, taxes and allocations to <u>general</u> corporate overhead.

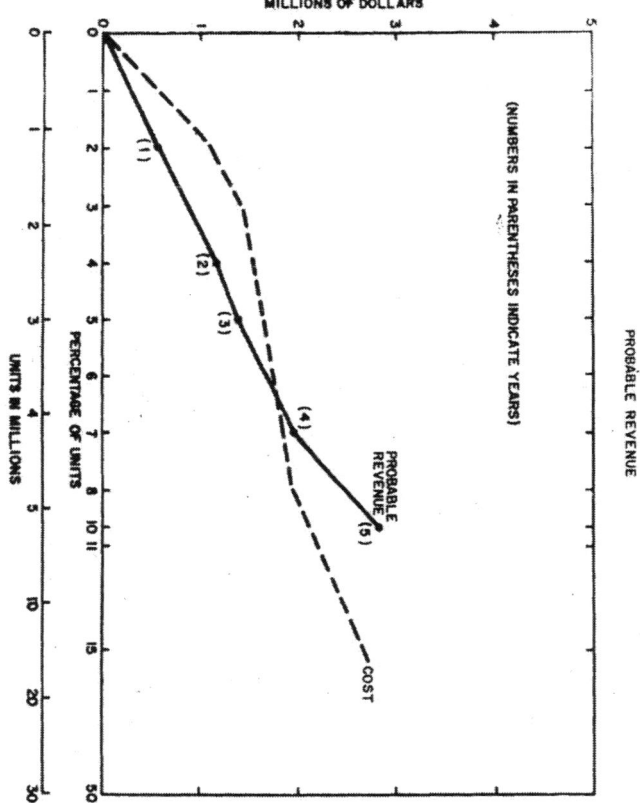

Exhibit 3a
PROBABLE REVENUE

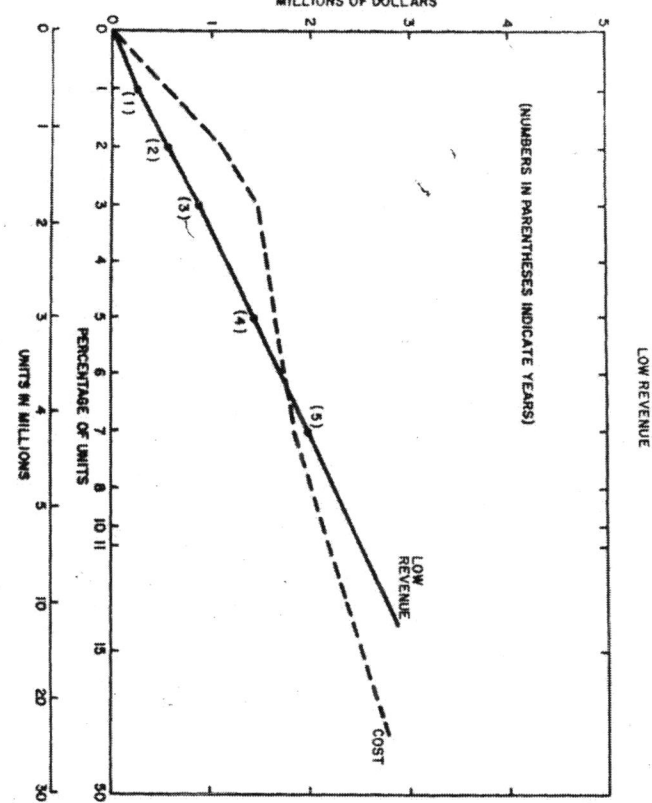

Exhibit 3b
LOW REVENUE

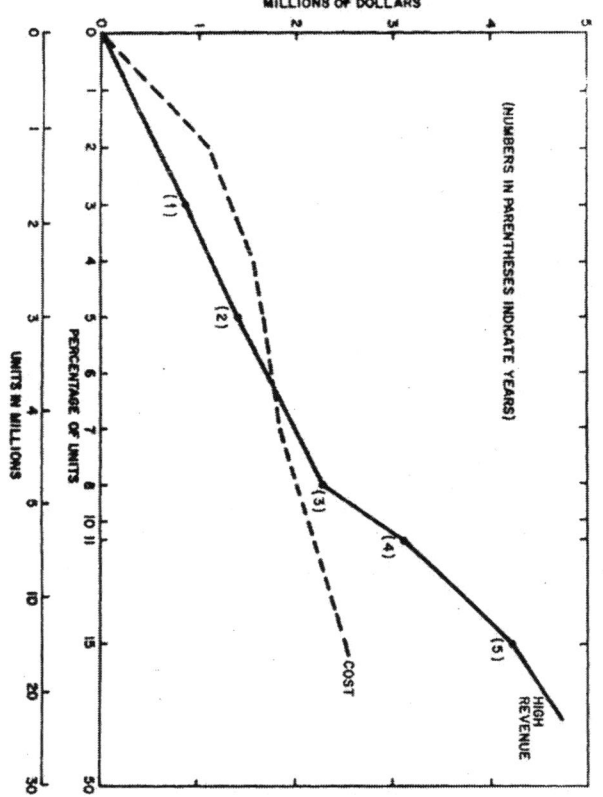

Exhibit 3c
HIGH REVENUE

Exhibit 4
ORGANIZATION CHART FOR NEW SOUL DIVISION

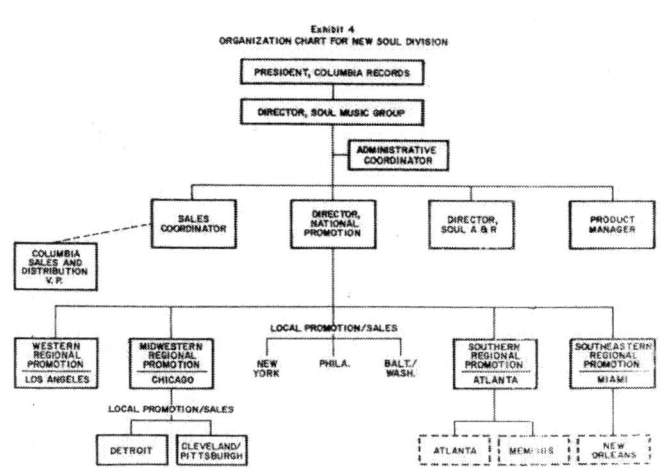

39

Exhibit 5
ENTRY PHASE OVERLAP

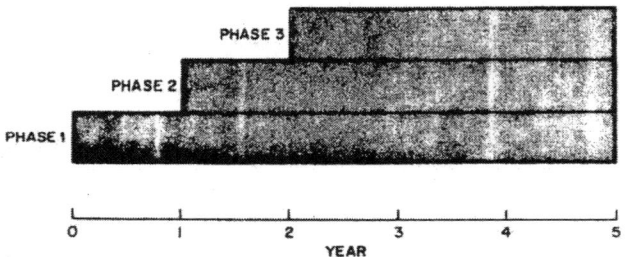

APPENDIX A

ESTIMATE OF SOUL MUSIC MARKET SIZE

The base from which the Soul market size estimate is determined is the total market estimate of approximately 175 million units each in singles and albums. For the years 1967-70 Soul music artists captured 22% of the RIAA audited Gold singles awards. Non-audited firms are assumed to add another 60% to sales giving Soul singles 35% of the total singles market. This percentage on extension gives:

$$.35 \times 175 = 61 \text{MM Units}$$

Market research data from CRG indicates that over the period 1967-71 Soul albums averaged 3% of total album sales. An examination of RIAA data for specific artists (i.e. those having Gold album awards) over this period suggests the CRG indications are too low by between 30 and 40 percent. (The error results from the composition of the panel used in developing CRG's data.) For the estimate it is assumed that Soul albums constitute about 7% of the total album market which is upon extension:

$$.07 \times 175 = 12.2 \text{MM Units}$$

To mitigate spurious accuracy, the above unit estimates are rounded to the figures presented in the text of:

Singles	60MM Units
Albums	12MM Units

The prices used in arriving at dollar volumes are given during the text discussion of market size.

A check was made using Billboard data on market share along with a confidential disclosure of one competitor's volume.

APPENDIX B

A broad based representative consumer survey was beyond the scope of the project. However, a telephone survey was undertaken in which 750 Black college students in the Boston area were contacted.

Black college students cannot be construed as being representative of the population of Soul record consumers. They are, however, a very important sub-segment of that group because:

a. They do make a significant number of purchases.

b. They have a great influence on tastes and trends within the Black community.

This survey was conducted by four college educated women from the Harvard Business School community. Analysis was performed through the use of the AQD (Analysis of Quantitative Data) package, which is a new program authored by Professor Robert O. Schlaiffer of the Harvard Business School.

The objectives of this survey were information oriented rather than action oriented. We have not reached any conclusions or made any recommendations based solely on this survey. For this reason, analysis was performed on only 278 of 750 responses. A disk file containing all 750 responses has been made available to you. Graphs and charts displaying information obtained are attached.

APPENDIX B (cont'd)

Age vs Factors Which Attract Consumer
To Rhythm & Blues

AGE	SOUND	ARTIST	LABEL	OTHER	TOTAL
16-18	96%	4%	*Results indicate label is unimportant in selection process	---	100%
18-20	89%	11%		---	100%
20-25	88%	9%		3%	100%
26-30	81%	19%		---	100%
31+	50%	38%		12%	100%

*Results indicate label is unimportant in selection process

*Number of Respondents to Survey by Age Group

Under 16 years of age		3
16-18	"	29
18-20	"	114
20-25	"	75
26-30	"	45
31+	"	12
	TOTAL	278

APPENDIX B (cont'd)

Age vs How Person First Gained Knowledge of a Record

AGE	RADIO	FRIEND	STORE	OTHER	TOTAL
16-18	86%	14%	---	---	100%
18-20	84%	14%	---	2%	100%
20-25	64%	23%	11%	2%	100%
26-30	61%	33%	3%	3%	100%
31+	63%	13%	12%	12%	100%

Age vs Outlet Where Records Purchased

AGE	SMALL LOCAL RECORD STORE	DEPT. STORE	BOOK STORE	DISCOUNT STORE	OTHER	TOTAL
16-18	55%	14%	17%	14%	--	100%
18-20	47%	17%	11%	25%	--	100%
20-25	35%	15%	24%	26%	--	100%
26-30	31%	19%	20%	30%	--	100%
31+	41%	0%	41%	18%	--	100%

APPENDIX B (cont'd)

Age vs Purchasing Outlet While in High School

AGE	SMALL STORE	DEPT. STORE	BOOK STORE	DISCOUNT STORE	OTHER	TOTAL
16-18	79%	11%	10%	--	--	100%
18-20	72%	15%	8%	1%	--	100%
20-25	61%	15%	14%	--	--	100%
26-30	68%	11%	7%	--	--	100%
31+	75%	--	--	--	25%	100%

* Some totals do not add up to 100% due to rounding.

Age vs Frequency of Purchase

AGE	WEEKLY	BI-WEEKLY	MONTHLY	EVERY FEW MONTHS	TOTAL
16-18	25%	14%	21%	32%	92%
18-20	18%	28%	27%	28%	101%
20-25	9%	27%	27%	38%	101%
26-30	13%	9%	28%	50%	100%
31+	13%	---	38%	50%	101%

* % do not equal 100% due to rounding.

APPENDIX B (cont'd)

Frequency of Purchase vs Amount Bought in a Month

TIME	2 RECORDS OR LESS	5 RECORDS OR LESS	10 RECORDS OR LESS	TOTAL
WEEKLY	16%	37%	47%	100%
BI-WEEKLY	22%	51%	27%	100%
MONTHLY	35%	41%	24%	100%
EVERY FEW MONTHS	55%	33%	10%	100%

ADDENDUM

Submitted by
Marnie Tattersall

At this research group's first meeting with CRG personnel, it was stated that CRG wants to be "Number One" in Soul music sales, profits, and number of artists on contract. This addendum is offered with some specific action recommendations which could be helpful, in conjunction with the recommendations in the body of this report in getting CRG to this goal.

**A best estimate of current market position
in this segment looks like this:**

Market Positions

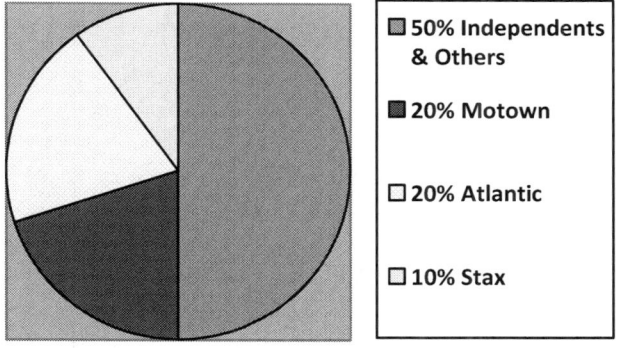

If CRG reaches its goal, the market will probably look like this:

Market Positions

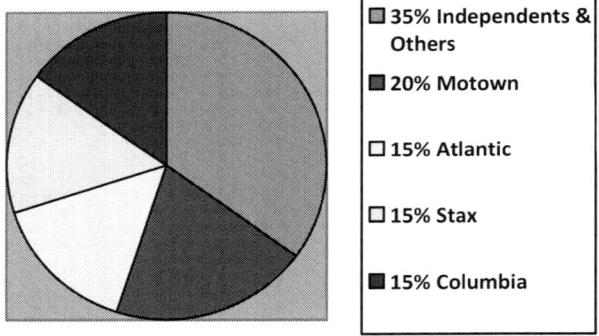

In essence, it is not unlikely that in order to be "Number One" in this segment, CGR will have to capture about 15 percent of it. This will not be easy, but it is not an impossible goal. If all CRG's resources are brought to bear in a concentrated effort, it is my feeling that CRG can reach this 15 percent in five years. In other words, CRG could be as large and dominant as Atlantic is in this segment by 1978.

To do this, however, will require higher market share goals and concurrent direct cost budgets than are presented in the body of this report. The following is what I see CRG being willing to spend and set as its yearly sales goals in order to produce and market the quality product which could make it "Number One" in five years.

Year	1	2	3	4	5
Market Size	$60MM	$64MM	$69MM	$74MM	$79MM
Estimated Level of Market Penetration	3%	5%	8%	11%	15%
Sales Volume	1.8MM	3.2MM	5.5MM	8.2MM	11.7MM
Contribution Available	840K	1,490K	2,570K	3,840K	5,600K
Less: Fixed Costs	830K	870K	915K	960K	1,010K
Historical Direct Costs	368K	658K	1,120K	1,590K	2,310K
Start-up Costs	200K	150K	--	--	--
	1,398K	1,670K	2,035K	2,550K	3,320K
Operating Profit (Loss)	(558K)	(180K)	535K	1,290K	*2,280K
Cumulative Profit (Loss)	(558K)	(738K)	(203K)	1,087K	3,367K
Unit Sales: Albums	350K	620K	1,070K	1,770K	2,570K
Single	1,750K	3,100K	5,350K	7,100K	10,300K

* Represents 19.5% operating profit on sales.

Assumptions: Same as in Exhibit 1.

With this goal in mind, the following are some of the kinds of actions which could be beneficial in terms of creating a more desirable image for CRG and in stimulating sales.

Program Director Convention
It was suggested by one of the program directors interviewed for this report, that if CRG is really serious about getting into the Soul market, it will have to start showing it. He suggested that a good way of establishing rapport between CRG and Black P.D.s and D.J.s would be to sponsor a conference for the ten or fifteen key Black P.D.s in the country. The purpose of the conference would be to announce CRG's desire to enter the market, to ask their advice, and in general to have a "rap session." The people he recommends inviting include Curt Shaw, WABQ Cleveland, the current president of NATRA; Bob Jones, KDIA San Francisco; and LeBaron Taylor, WDAS Philadelphia.

Radio Station Relations
Some of the things being done to gain favorable rapport by other companies in this market—in lieu of illegal inducements—which were cited by station personnel as being desirable include:

- Occasional visits by artists and record company executives

- Purchase of air time to advertise current product or concerts

- Purchase of advertising space on the station's complimentary "Hit List"

- Use of stations D.J.s as M.C.s for concerts

- Invitations to local press parties

Concerts
As mentioned in the report, exposure has been and continues to remain a real problem for Black artists. While expenses for a touring Black act do not differ significantly from a White act, there is still usually a sizable difference in audience. This makes promoting Black concerts a usually much less profitable proposal, which has led to a dearth of popularly priced live Black performances across the country. There are several things that CRG can do to help its Black artists in this area.

- Help out with concert tour expenses
- Recommend top flight booking and management agencies
- Work with and encourage Black concert promoters
- Sponsor or co-sponsor free or token-charge concerts
    - other record companies, i.e. ABC are already doing this
    - it is rumored that companies such as Coca-Cola and 7-Up are interested in this area
- Encourage the billing of Soul acts with Pop acts
    - i.e. Van Morrison with the Dramatics

- very little of this is being done to date—with the result that White audiences are seldom exposed to live Soul performances.

Soul Train

Television is considered a White medium. There is increasing pressure for minority programming from Nicolas Johnson, FCC Commissioner to the recent Black caucus on media. The result of this White orientation is that few Black artists get national television exposure; yet television is such a powerful medium for exposure that a recent BILLBOARD article suggests that television spots may become tomorrow's medium for advertising new musical acts and albums.

It is my feeling that the young White audience of today is not half as hung-up on seeing and "digging" Black artists as are the older White generation who control television programing. Thus, if more Black-oriented programs and Black artists were given national exposure, the effect on ratings may not be as detrimental as feared.

With CRG entering the Black market, it would be in its, and, therefore, CBS Incorporated's best interest to do what it can to influence and encourage more Black exposure on CBS television in particular, and on other television networks and stations in general. (It is interesting to note that NBC and RCA worked together to bring out color television.)

A case in point is *Soul Train*—an independently produced Black "Dick Clark" type show out of Los Angeles. Because it has been refused by the national networks, it is showing on a haphazard basis in whatever cities it can find a marginal station willing to program it. In Boston, for example, it is programmed on Channel 56—where it is gathering a significant audience—despite the fact that many potential viewers do not have televisions which receive more than twelve channels.

Were CBS television to syndicate this show, with only minor alterations—such as using several different cities for location, and including occasional White 'Soul' acts—it could pick up a substantial young Black, and White, national audience. It is only a matter of time before some network picks it up.

There is also ample demand for a television concert series; the poor sound quality argument not withstanding—it is no worse than most radios. One evidence of this is the positive sales that CRG experienced when it programmed parts of its annual promotion movie on Seattle, Washington, television. It is rumored that a sizable department store chain in New England would like to sponsor a similar show but has not been able to find the material.

Thus, it is essential that CRG realize the potential power of television to cultivate the audience for Soul music, and to positively influence Soul record sales.

Radio
Again, in reference to the exposure problem as well as the payola scare, it should be realized that CBS Radio owns seven AM and seven FM stations, as well as providing programming for some 246 radio stations across the country. None of this is Black programming, even though a considerable opportunity exists for more Black-oriented radio programming. (A separate report is available on this subject.)

Were CBS Radio to offer Black programming of the kind desired—which would include more album exposure—the programming would be profitable. CRG could benefit by having a radio outlet which—while not doing it any favors—at least could not refuse to play 'Columbia' records; and album airplay will generate significant album sales over singles airplay which is the vogue on most current Black radio.

"Discount Record Stores"
Mom and Pop record stores are particularly important to the Soul music market because a much higher percent of Soul product is purchased through them than is the case with White or Pop music. One of the basic reasons for this is that the geographic dispersion and travel patterns for Blacks are different from those of Whites. Thus, a large portion of the Black record-buying public does not have the same access to rack outlets as do Whites.

Currently CRG owns record retail outlets in various cities, but none in the ghetto areas of these cities. At first glance it would seem that establishing these stores in ghetto areas would only succeed in putting the Mom and Pops out of business, while creating unneeded ill-will and trouble. Nevertheless, it would be very desirable for CRG to have such outlets, because it could have a direct pulse on what is happening at the Black retail level—a pulse so important that Atlantic and Motown are in daily contact with their key inner-city retailers.

A way of getting around the ill-will that could be generated by CRG ownership of ghetto record stores would be to establish stores on a franchise basis. An arrangement could be worked out whereby young Blacks who are looking for opportunities to own their own businesses, but do not have the capital, could manage the stores and pay for them out of earnings.

If the owner/managers belonged to the community in which they set up shop, they would have the advantage of knowing the community, little opposition could be voiced because these young people are as entitled as the Mom and Pops to start their own business, the venture would help build Black capital, the community would benefit from lower prices and wider variety, and CRG would not only get the information it needed, but its image as a leader in minority business development would be enhanced.

Public and Industry Image

As mentioned in the report, CRG does have a real image problem with regard to entering the Black market. This image can and should be changed, but it will take some doing.

Following is an example of what one other company in the business is doing. The company is Atlantic Records—part of the Kinney group that is now considered such a powerful threat to CRG's total market dominance.

- Atlantic invariably buys a table for the company when a Black station recommends a local Black charity event.
- Last Christmas, Atlantic gave away three thousand dollars worth of turkeys to the poor in Philadelphia through WDAS radio. The turkeys were purchased from a local Black turkey grower and said simply, "Season's Best Wishes from WDAS and Atlantic Records."

The positive feedback that is generated at the station level and from the recipients for these types of action is phenomenal. CRG will have to start thinking about engaging in similar "public spirited" endeavors. If not for the simple reason that these actions should be taken, then they should be done for defensive strategic reasons—besides, they are tax deductible.

The concern that record companies should start putting back some of the money they have been taking out of the community for so long is getting strong enough that it is rumored a coalition in Harlem is being organized to boycott record companies that do not engage in this.

These are some of the things CRG should consider doing. One word of caution though—they must be done tastefully.

- Support Black charity functions
- Contribute food to the poor through radio stations and perhaps the Panthers.
- Establish minority music scholarships as grants.
    1. These could be set up at schools such as New England Conservatory or Julliard.
    2. They could be administered by CRG to promising individuals, i.e. winners from the Apollo amateur contests, so that they could spend a year or two taking lessons from masters or traveling to countries such as in Africa to be exposed to native African music. The musicians chosen, and the world of music could only benefit from this type of opportunity; not to mention the rich potential for future CRG artists that this could offer.

In closing, I would like to add, Black music stands to gain as much as CRG from a whole-hearted CRG attempt to participate in the market. It would be a shame for CRG not to live up to its potential.

Made in the USA
Middletown, DE
20 July 2017